101+ Greatest Quotes on Happiness, Success and Motivation from famous people around the world

Sneha Rawat

Introduction

This book is the collection of most powerful words ever used by greatest minds around the world. It contains the best of the wisdom they got during their lives. Words have power. Admit it or not words can make you feel the happiest man on earth or the saddest person ever lived. The whole law of attraction theory revolve around the power of words.

As Tony Robbins says Words have the power to start wars or create peace, destroy relationships or strengthen them. How we feel about anything is shaped by the meaning we attach to it. The words you consciously or unconsciously select to describe a situation immediately change what it means to you and thus how you feel.

"Language shapes our behavior and each word we use is imbued with multitudes of personal meaning. The right words spoken in the right way can bring us love, money, and respect, while the wrong words—or even the right words spoken in the wrong way—can lead to a country to war. We must carefully orchestrate our speech if we want to achieve our goals and bring our dreams to fruition."
—Dr. Andrew Newberg, Words Can Change Your Brain

Throughout human history, great leaders have used the power of words to transform our emotions, to enlist us in their causes, and to shape the course of destiny.

As Jim Rohn always said there are 5 major pieces of life: Philosophy, Attitude, Activity, Result, and Lifestyle.

And to create any change in life you must start by refining your philosophy. You cannot change your destination overnight, but you can change your direction overnight.

These quotes are collected in such a way that they will help you to refine your philosophy.

Start each day with a powerful word of wisdom and let it guide you to take action, overcome fear, boost your self-esteem, create success.

"I've missed more than 9000 shots in my career. I've lost almost 300 games. 26 times, I've been trusted to take the game winning shot and missed. I've failed over and over and over again in my life. And that is why I succeed."
— Michael Jordan

"Happiness is the meaning and the purpose of life, the whole aim, and end of human existence"
— Aristotle

"Strength does not come from winning. Your struggles develop your strengths. When you go through hardships and decide not to surrender, that is strength."
— Arnold Schwarzenegger

"Knowing others is intelligence; knowing yourself is true wisdom. Mastering others is strength; mastering yourself is true power. If you realize that you have enough, you are truly rich."
— Tao Te

"I have not failed. I've just found 10,000 ways that won't work."
— Thomas A. Edison

"If you want happiness for an hour —
take a nap.
If you want happiness for a day —
go fishing.
If you want happiness for a year —
inherit a fortune.
If you want happiness for a lifetime
help someone else."
— Chinese Proverb

"Do your future self a favor and work hard now."
— J. Cole

"There is no greater agony than bearing an untold story inside you."
— Maya Angelou, I Know Why the Caged Bird Sings

"The greatest glory in living lies not in never falling, but in rising every time we fall."
— Ralph Waldo Emerson

"Everyone wants to live on top of the mountain, but all the happiness and growth occurs while you're climbing it."
— Andy Rooney

"I like criticism. It makes you strong."
— LeBron James

"The greatest sin is to think yourself
weak"
— Swami Vivekananda, Pearls of
Wisdom

"Success means having the courage,
the determination, and the will to
become the person you believe you were
meant to be."
— George Sheehan

"A disciplined mind leads to
happiness, and an undisciplined mind
leads to suffering."
— Dalai Lama xiv, The Art of
Happiness

"All our dreams can come true if we have the courage to pursue them."
— Walt Disney

"No one can make you feel inferior without your consent."
— Eleanor Roosevelt, This is My Story

"The secret of success is learning how to use pain and pleasure instead of having pain and pleasure use you. If you do that, you're in control of your life. If you don't, life controls you."
— Tony Robbins

"Happiness is not the absence of problems, it's the ability to deal with them."
— Steve Maraboli

"If you really want to do something, you'll find a way. If you don't, you'll find an excuse."
– Jim Rohn

"Courage is the discovery that you may not win, and trying when you know you can lose."
–Tom Krause

"I cannot give you the formula for success, but I can give you the formula for failure which is: Try to please everybody."
– Herbert B. Swope

"Happiness is when what you think, what you say, and what you do are in harmony."
– Mahatma Gandhi

"If you're going through hell keep
going."
– Winston Churchill

"Excellence is not a singular act, but a
habit. You are what you repeatedly do."
– Shaquille ONeal

"The test of success is not what you do
when you are on top. Success is how high
you bounce when you hit the bottom."
– George S. Patton Jr.

"The happiest people do not
necessarily have the best things.
They simply appreciate the things they
have."
– Warren Buffett

"A truly strong person does not need the approval of others any more than a lion needs the approval of sheep."
— Vernon Howard

"Limitations live only in our minds. But if we use our imaginations, our possibilities become limitless."
— Jamie Paolinetti

"Small daily improvements over time lead to stunning results."
— Robin Sharma

"Happiness is like a kiss. you must share it to enjoy it."
— Bernard Meltzer

"Tough times never last, but tough people do."
— Robert H. Schuller

"...God's love is so real that He created you to prove it."
— Nick Vujicic, Life Without Limits

"Only those who dare to fail greatly can ever achieve greatly."
— Robert F. Kennedy

"There are no great things, only small things with great love. Happy are those."
— Mother Teresa

"If you can't fly then run if you can't run then walk if you can't walk then crawl, but whatever you do you have to keep moving forward."
— Martin Luther King Jr.

"If you only do what you know you can do- you never do very much."
— Tom Krause

"Success is simple. Do what's right, the right way, at the right time."
— Arnold H. Glasgow

"The tough truth about life is that some things just take time. Most people aren't strong enough to deal with that fact."
— Tai Lopez

"Happiness is not something readymade. It comes from your own actions."
– Dalai Lama

"Don't take rest after your first victory because if you fail in second, more lips are waiting to say that your first victory was just luck."
– Dr. APJ Abdul Kalam

"Do not spoil what you have by desiring what you have not; remember that what you now have was once among the things you only hoped for."
– Epicurus

"The greatest mistake you can make in life is to be continually fearing you will make one."
– Elbert Hubbard

"Happy people are beautiful. They become like a mirror and they reflect that happiness."
– Drew Barrymore

"Sometimes you don't realize your own strength until you come face to face with your greatest weakness."
—Susan Gale

"Nearly all men can stand adversity, but if you want to test a man's character, give him power."
– Abraham Lincoln

"You know what's better than building things up in your imagination? Building things up in real life."
— Ryan Holiday, The Obstacle Is the Way

"The greater part of our misery or unhappiness is determined not by our circumstance but by our disposition."
— Martha Washington

"I fear not the man who has practiced 10,000 kicks once, but I fear the man who had practiced one kick 10,000 times."
— Bruce Lee

"A wise man makes his own decisions, an ignorant man follows public opinion"
— Chinese Proverbs

"When we give ourselves permission to fail, we, at the same time, give ourselves permission to excel."
— Eloise Ristad

"Happiness doesn't depend on any external conditions, it is governed by our mental attitude."
— Dale Carnegie

"The good life is to be earned with hard work and sacrifice."
— Dr T.P.Chia

"Real power comes not from hate, but from truth."
— Seth Grahame-Smith, Abraham Lincoln: Vampire Hunter

"Victory is sweetest when you've known defeat."
– Malcolm S. Forbes

"Happiness Is Not A Goal... It's A By-Product of A Life Well Lived."
– Eleanor Roosevelt

"Strength is Life, Weakness is Death.
– Swami Vivekananda

"A wise man changes his mind, a fool never"
– Spanish Proverb

"Action is the foundational key to all success."
– Pablo Picasso

"Action May Not Always Bring Happiness, But There Is No Happiness Without Action."
– Benjamin Disraeli

"Strength and growth come only through continuous effort and struggle."
—Napoleon Hill

"Love is a gift of one's inner most soul to another so both can be whole."
– Buddha

"Criticism precedes admiration and—like it or not—goes hand in hand with success."
– Grant Cardone, The 10X Rule

"The measure of the moral worth of a man is his happiness. The better the man, the more happiness. Happiness is the synonym of well-being."
— Bruce Lee

"Great minds discuss ideas; average minds discuss events; small minds discuss people."
— Eleanor Roosevelt

"Wise are they who have learned these truths: Trouble is temporary. Time is tonic. Tribulation is a test tube."
— William Arthur Ward

"Success is stumbling from failure to failure with no loss of enthusiasm."
— Winston Churchill

"Love and compassion are necessities, not luxuries. Without them, humanity cannot survive."
— Dalai Lama XIV, The Art of Happiness

"I find that the harder I work, the more luck I seem to have."
— Thomas Jefferson

"The wise man questions the wisdom of others because he questions his own, the foolish man because it is different from his own."
— Leo Stein

"We will either find a way or make one."
— Hannibal (247-182 BC), Carthaginian General

"Think Less Live More."
— Shelley Row

"Nothing in the world is more common
than unsuccessful people with talent,
leave the house before you find
something worth staying in for. "
— Banksy

"It is characteristic of wisdom not to
do desperate things."
— Henry David Thoreau

"The first step toward success is taken
when you refuse to be a captive of the
environment in which you first find
yourself."
— Mark Caine

"We all have inner demons to fight, we call these demons, fear and hatred and anger. If you do not conquer them then a life of one hundred years is a tragedy. If you do, then a life of a single day can be a triumph."
— Yip Man

"You must expect great things of yourself before you can do them."
— Michael Jordan

"We can be knowledgeable with other men's knowledge, but we cannot be wise with other men's wisdom."
— Michel de Montaigne

"One who fears failure limits his activities. Failure is only the opportunity to more intelligently begin again."
— Henry Ford

"We tend to forget that happiness doesn't come as a result of getting something we don't have, but rather of recognizing and appreciating what we do have."
— Frederick Keonig

"If you don't design your own life plan, chances are you'll fall into someone else's plan. And guess what they have planned for you? Not much."
— Jim Rohn

"Wisdom does not come overnight"
— African Proverb

"Every problem can be solved as long as they use common sense and apply the right research and techniques."
— Daymond John

"Remember That The Happiest People
Are Not Those Getting More, But Those
Giving More."
– H. Jackson Brown, Jr.

"Real difficulties can be overcome; it is
only the imaginary ones that are
unconquerable."
– Theodore N. Vail

"The fool wonders, the wise man asks."
– Benjamin Disraeli

"Failure shows us the way—by showing
us what isn't the way."
– Ryan Holiday, The Obstacle Is the
Way

"People love others not for who they are but for how they make them feel"
— Irwin Federman

"If you are not willing to risk the usual you will have to settle for the ordinary." -
— Jim Rohn

"If you want to live a happy life, tie it to a goal, not to people or things."
— Albert Einstein

"You may have to fight a battle more than once to win it."
— Margaret Thatcher

"Thousands of candles can be lit from a single candle, and the life of the candle will not be shortened. Happiness never decreases by being shared."
— Buddha

"Start small and dream big."
— Robert Kiyosaki

"The oldest trees often bear the sweetest fruit"
— German Proverb

"A person's success in life can usually be measured by the number of uncomfortable conversations he or she is willing to have."
— Timothy Ferriss

"Happiness comes of the capacity to
feel deeply, to enjoy simply, to think
freely, to risk life, to be needed."
— Storm Jameson

"There are two ways of exerting one's
strength: one is pushing down, the other
is pulling up."
— Booker T. Washington

"Many receive advice, only the wise
profit from it."
— Publilius Syrus

"The greater the struggle the more
glorious the triumph"
— Nick Vujicic

"Nothing can bring you happiness but yourself."
— Ralph Waldo Emerson

"It's not what you say out of your mouth that determines your life, it's what you whisper to yourself that has the most power!"
— Robert Kiyosaki

"Silence and reserve will give anyone a reputation for wisdom."
— Myrtle Reed

"Unless we have something worth dying for, we've nothing worth living for."
— Francine Rivers, A Voice in the Wind

"Successful Investing takes time, discipline and patience. No matter how great the talent or effort, some things just take time: You can't produce a baby in one month by getting nine women pregnant."
— Warren Buffett

"It's far better to buy a wonderful company at a fair price than a fair company at a wonderful price."
— Warren Buffett

"The question I ask myself like almost every day is, 'Am I doing the most important thing I could be doing?' ... Unless I feel like I'm working on the most important problem that I can help with, then I'm not going to feel good about how I'm spending my time."
— From Marcia Amidon Lusted's biography Mark Zuckerberg: Facebook Creator

"Innovation distinguishes between a leader and a follower."
— Steve Jobs

"It's not knowing what to do; it's doing what you know."
— Tony Robbins

"A bad strategy will fail no matter how good your information is, and lame execution will stymie a good strategy. If you do enough things poorly, you will go out of business."
— Bill Gates

"If you can remember why you started, then you will know why you must continue."
— Chris Burkmenn

All you want to achieve is possible,
now all you need is to work hard and
Leave no stone unturned.
I wish you the best of luck on your
journey with most inspiring lines from
Walter D. Wintle.

"If you think you are beaten, you
are.
If you think you dare not, you
don't.
If you'd like to win but think you
can't,
It's almost certain you won't.
Life's battles don't always go
To the stronger or faster man,
But sooner or later, the man who
wins
Is the man who thinks he can."

Made in the USA
Columbia, SC
30 November 2018